Journey into Loving You

Author: Lisa McTavis LMSW
Editor: Suzen Stover James, ACSW, LISW

BALBOA.
PRESS

A DIVISION OF HAY HOUSE

Balboa Press books may be ordered through booksellers or by contacting:

Balboa Press
A Division of Hay House
1663 Liberty Drive
Bloomington, IN 47403
www.balboapress.com
1-(877) 407-4847

Because of the dynamic nature of the Internet, any web addresses or links contained in this book may have changed since publication and may no longer be valid. The views expressed in this work are solely those of the author and do not necessarily reflect the views of the publisher, and the publisher hereby disclaims any responsibility for them.

The author of this book does not dispense medical advice or prescribe the use of any technique as a form of treatment for physical, emotional, or medical problems without the advice of a physician, either directly or indirectly. The intent of the author is only to offer information of a general nature to help you in your quest for emotional and spiritual well-being. In the event you use any of the information in this book for yourself, which is your constitutional right, the author and the publisher assume no responsibility for your actions.

Any people depicted in stock imagery provided by Thinkstock are models,
and such images are being used for illustrative purposes only.
Certain stock imagery © Thinkstock.

Printed in the United States of America.

ISBN: 978-1-4525-7838-5 (sc)
ISBN: 978-1-4525-7839-2 (e)

Library of Congress Control Number: 2013913065

Balboa Press rev. date: 7/30/2013

Table of Contents

Forewords

In your hands you hold, "Journey into Loving You". It will be your road map to assist with your explorations into self- awareness, enlightenment, and self-acceptance… with the destination of having a sense of wholeness you may never have envisioned.

Artfully and creatively written by Lisa McTavis, LMSW, a skillful clinical social worker in the New Mexico area, the book exemplifies a beautiful blend of her personal discoveries and insights. Ms. McTavis will adeptly guide you through your own personal journey, whatever you choose the journey to be.

You will have the opportunity to discover how to love, forgive and completely accept yourself. The practical exercises which assist one in accepting and working through stressful and anxiety provoking emotions are invaluable.

I have had the honor and privilege of witnessing the evolution of this book. Thank you to a very beautiful woman.

"No one saves us but ourselves. No one can and no one may. We ourselves must walk the path"   *Buddha*

Enjoy your journey!
Suzen Stover James, ACSW, LISW

In the book you are about to read, Lisa McTavis offers a template for self-understanding and self-love. Template derives from temple, a house of worship building being worthy. Lisa uses beams of acceptance, forgiveness, validation, and agency to construct an elightening and enlivening structure for self-worth.

I hope you enjoy the journey.

Avi Kriechman, M.D.

I think that all too often, taking care of ourselves becomes confused with the idea of selfishness or self-centeredness. From my perspective, that kind of confusion is the source of many of the problems we face as humans. And, when we become caretakers of others, as the vast majority of us become, that confusion can be even more damaging and unhealthy for those we care about.

Lisa McTavis' *Journey into Loving You* does an enlightening job of showing us how to get back on task or make a start on how to view one's own welfare as a first step in making our own lives, the lives of the ones we love and ultimately, our communities more healthy and places where all of us can meet our potential. By reminding us that acceptance, love and approval come from within, she educates many of us around the idea that we are the source of those positive ingredients for a life that can be fulfilling for us as individuals and for those around us.

Lisa has a very solid foundation of experience and knowledge upon which to make her recommendations. She hails from the profession of clinical social work and academically has established a solid knowledge base and an excellent set of therapeutic skills that she uses very successfully with her clients. Knowledge and skills are nothing and have no power at all without values that are focused in a positive direction. The values of self-determination and a focus on strengths rather than weaknesses are truly evident throughout this comprehensive work.

As a clinical social worker, I (and I would venture to say the majority of my colleagues) adhere to the concept of empowerment. Professionals recognize that the goal of clinical interventions (therapy, counseling, case management, advocacy, etc) is not to provide services - even though it may look like that is exactly what we are doing. The goal is to empower others to have more control over their own behaviors and over what is going on around them in their environment. This volume adheres to that perspective on how humans gain control over their lives and does it in a very successful manner.

George W. Mercer, LISW

Preface

I didn't have the intention to write the book, Journey into Loving You. The book began to write itself and I followed along. All that is in the book is what I learned along the way of loving and accepting myself and refining the techniques as I worked with clients. I wanted to keep the book as simple and distilled down as I could. I feel the more simple I can keep these ideas and techniques the easier they will be to understand and use in daily living. You will notice this is not a large book, it is however powerful and would guide the reader to go slow through the chapters and do all the exercises to get the full impact of what this book offers.

As I moved along my own journey into loving and accepting myself help was always available when I was ready to move deeper into it. The universe seemed to be supporting me and bringing me exactly what I needed, when I needed it. As I moved deeper into the connection within me, I began to understand I was tapping into something very powerful, my own inner wisdom. I found the door opened inward and expanded from there. This was a turning point in my journey where I began to guide me from within. I believe the most important work we can do is to love and accept ourselves. The love really is already there, we simply have to remove the layers of illusions we have picked up along our own unique journeys that limit it us from experiencing it. Now that the book is finished I am so very grateful to all that I am, for I know I really was writing it for me. It is my hope that when you read the book, you will find it was written for you too.

Acknowledgement

How do you say thank you to someone who has supported, encouraged, inspired, taught, and assisted you on so many levels? I could not find the words to convey my gratitude to my editor, mentor, and friend Suzen Stover James, ACSW, LISW. I thought she might appreciate a multi-cultural approach: Thank you, Wiliwni, Dankie, Baie Dankie, Falemenderit shumë, Qagaasakuq, متشكّرين, մերսի, Barkalla, 謝謝, Chi yakōkilih chitoh, Merci, Tausend Dank, Grazzie, Gratias Tibi ago, Takk, Tapadh leibh, and Muchas gracias.

I don't want to try to imagine what doing this project without you would have been like, you are the perfect editor, and I was so very blessed to have you.

I was blessed to have 3 of my professors from graduate school write the forewards for this book. Thank you Avi, George, and dear Suzen again, you guys are amazing and I was so fortunate to be able to learn from all of you. Thank you to Yvonne D. Hall MD, you are inspiring. Thank you to my beautiful daughter for the privilege of being your mom. I believe everyone who has crossed my path has contributed to my understanding of how to love and accept myself and are far too many to begin to list them here but send a deeply felt thank you to all of you.

Introduction

Many of us have been taught a lie. A lie that says everything which is good and worthwhile is outside of you and you must find it there externally. The lie says that all acceptance, validation, love, approval and joy must be given to you, by someone else and found somewhere else. You are not alone in accepting this lie, the majority of the world population also shares this belief in this lie with you. The lie is, it is not outside of you, or with anyone else, or somewhere else. The truth is all the love, acceptance, validation, approval, and joy is waiting for you within.

Whenever you look outside of yourself for any of these things, the source will always be conditional. Conditional upon how the other person perceives and thinks about you, how they feel about themselves, and what is happening outside of them. When you look for these things within, the source becomes unconditional through your own love and acceptance of yourself. It is a journey, a walk which takes you not to a destination but a way of life. Often when you search for love and validation outside of yourself, it comes with a price tag. The cost results from the expectation, "since I helped you, you now must help me". A dynamic created by "I did this for you, and now I want you to do this for me". Whatever the "this" is, becomes unique to the particular situation but is usually owed.

What if you could fulfill you, by validating yourself through acceptance, love, approval, and joy that you never had to look outside yourself for? Surprisingly, this was always there, a never ending, overflowing source that was always ready for you to tap into. Such a thing would empower you, create confidence and the ability to be in any situation, with any type of person, and you would no longer need them to empower you because you were already doing it for yourself. When you did receive love, acceptance, validation, approval, or joy from another, it became a sharing experience that was not required to meet a need. It is my hope in sharing what I have learned on this journey that I may offer you support along yours. It is a beautiful thing indeed.

Take the quiz before you read the book and the same quiz will be available after you read the book to determine how your perceptions have changed or remained the same. Answer each question with the first response that comes into your mind.

Do you feel ignored when no one is paying attention to you?

Do you feel you have to protect yourself around others?

If you feel someone else has let you down, rejected or betrayed you, do you pull away from everyone else around you as well?

When you are around others do you sometimes act differently depending upon who you are with?

How safe do you feel you can be who you really are around others?

When something upsets you, do you feel tired and/or weak?

Do you feel upset with yourself if you make a mistake?

Do you feel judged by others if you make a mistake?

Do you feel that you cannot trust others?

Do you feel you can trust yourself?

Have you ever felt you had something to share with others but decided not to because you were worried how they would react?

Have you ever had a frustration in your life but you pretended like everything was ok?

Has someone in your life made you feel cold and distant?

Have you felt unsure or insecure about who you are?

When you are getting dressed in the morning what determines what you are going to wear for that day? *1. I want to look good and impress others around me. 2. I want to be comfortable with what I choose?*

Do you believe about yourself *1. I must follow all the rules around me and do what others think I should. 2. I am ok if I am fitting in with the world. 3. I do what I feel is appropriate regardless of what others are doing around me.*

The purpose of my life is *1. I am growing and learning how to be perfect. 2. Embracing each experience 3. Learning how to succeed and fit in with the world around me.*

I believe I am lovable when *1. I have earned someone else's love. 2. I am doing all the right things. 3. I do nothing.*

Chapter 1

Acceptance

Why would you want to love yourself? I will tell you I found it the most difficult thing I have ever done, and also the most empowering. I found accepting who I was the easiest place to start. How do you accept all of you when there are parts and pieces even you have judged as wrong or inappropriate?

It starts with the understanding that in every moment you have done the best you can and it is good enough. We live in a world of relationships. Relationships with ourselves, families, friends, co-workers, fellow students, and within the communities we live in. Each relationship we encounter on any given day is also being affected by outside influences happening around those individuals. We are all interconnected and interacting on varying levels daily. This leads to my point of we do the best we can. We do the best we can when we consider what is happening outside of us and within us.

In each moment we are interacting in relationship dynamics and many things are affecting us greatly. We do the best we can with all of these interactions. When I say the best we can, I do not mean the best we idealize ourselves as being capable of. None of us can operate at that level for any extended period of time. If we did, we would burn ourselves out quickly. To operate on a daily consistent level, we do the best we can in each of these situations. I found I had a bar that was raised to the level of what I considered I was capable of. This bar represented what expectations I had for myself, and what I had been capable of attaining in previous experiences along with belief systems in place. I also had to reach this bar in order for me to feel I had done the best I could. The problem with the bar is most days it was unreachable.

Maybe once or twice I had reached high enough and was able to exert enough effort to reach that level but that was when the situations outside of me and within were optimal to support me in that. The expectation of me to reach the bar on a daily level was unattainable and once I could create the awareness of that bar, I also could start to lower it to a more reasonable level. When is it good enough for you? When have you done enough or behaved in a certain way that you feel it is good enough?

I found it helpful to put the same expectation I had for myself onto someone else. I would look at an action and all of the outside influences, as well as any emotions I had at the time and then ask, "Can I expect so and so to be able to do better?" To say we do the best we can and it is good enough, is a choice we can make to see it is "good enough". It is what we have in each moment and to expect more from ourselves only sets the bar higher than we can achieve. I would tell you that you can keep criticizing yourself, beating yourself up for what you have or haven't done but I also would ask you how helpful has the criticism been? Do you feel better when you criticize yourself or worse? What we take down, we also hold down and then are unable to get back up and move forward.

Exercises

Think about a time in the past when you have judged your actions as wrong or inappropriate. Write the situation below. Try to describe the situation as if you were an observer who was not directly involved in the situation.

_____

_____

_____

_____

_____

_____

_____

_____

What expectation did have for yourself in this situation. What could you have done differently that you would have felt was good enough?

_____
_____
_____
_____
_____
_____
_____
_____
_____
_____

What were some of the outside influences or factors happening at the time? Outside includes people, events, or situations outside of you, which were directly influencing what was happening. Example: I was late for work and was worried I was going to get yelled at by my boss. My car wouldn't start and I had to wait for someone to charge my battery.

_____
_____
_____
_____
_____
_____
_____
_____
_____
_____

What emotions were present at the time of the situation? What were you feeling before, during, and after the situation? Example: I was anxious and becoming more nervous as the situation progressed.

_____

_____

_____

_____

_____

_____

_____

_____

_____

_____

Now consider the dynamics or outside influences happening at the time. I also ask you to consider what emotions you were feeling at the time. As you bring the outside influences in and your emotions into consideration, do you really feel your actions could have been different? It is important to consider all of what was happening at the time, including emotions which were in place during the situation. It is easier to criticize our own actions once the situation has passed and we are reflecting back on those actions and we often do not remember all that was affecting us including what we were feeling at the time. If we recall our feelings at the time, we can obtain a clearer picture of the influences that were affecting us. It is also important to bring compassion or understanding to this evaluation. Is it reasonable to believe or accept, considering all that was happening, that you did do the best you could in that particular situation?

Remember it is not about the best you are capable of but rather the best you could do then. Was the expectation you had for yourself reasonable or attainable in that situation? Can you place someone else in the exact situation and expect her/

him to rise to the level you are asking yourself to? It will also be useful to become aware of where you have placed your bar of expectation and if necessary, lower your expectations of yourself to a level more reasonably attainable. Please now write how you now feel about yourself in this situation.

_____

_____

_____

_____

_____

_____

_____

_____

_____

_____

_____

This exercise is designed to help you to accept your actions and yourself. This exercise is not designed to excuse any behaviors you do not wish to repeat, or to not take appropriate responsibility for your choices. It is the acceptance of who we are that allows the compassion or understanding to emerge. The compassion allows us to be authentic with ourselves and empowers us in the acceptance of the fact we are doing the best we can in each moment. We also can choose to do things differently in our future experiences.

The hindsight vision of how we have managed situations previously provides us with a tool which allows us to use the information to make different choices. The hindsight can be a double edged sword if we judge our actions and expect ourselves to have the insight we just obtained from the experience prior to having the experience. The expectation for us to know, what we do not know, does not serve us, nor does it help us in self acceptance. Each moment provides us with the opportunity to choose the belief we do the best we can every moment and to accept it is "good enough".

Useful tips:

Please use this exercise as many times as you need to, including all the experiences you have had which you are still carrying guilt or shame for anything you have done. When I began using this technique I found myself using it up to 100 times a day on some days. With practice and daily use, I found it became an automatic process for me throughout my daily experiences. It also may be helpful while you are initially doing this to go back and review weekly or daily experiences and try to create awareness of when you were judging yourself and use the technique to create self acceptance in those situations.

Please be reminded to be compassionate with yourself while you are changing the old patterning of not accepting yourself or your actions to the new pattern of accepting yourself or your actions. The old patterning of not accepting you have been in place for a long time and patience with yourself through the changes will be of the most service.

I found it helpful to start observing myself as much as I could when I first began using this. When I found myself in a situation where I began to judge myself as wrong, I reminded myself I was doing the best I could in this situation and it was good enough. As soon as I had the opportunity after the situation, I would look at the influences occurring in the situation. I found I really was doing the best I could in that moment. I again reminded myself to be compassionate through the changes.

You might find it useful to allow yourself at least one to two weeks to work on this Chapter before moving to Chapter 2. Journaling about any of your experiences, thoughts, interpretations, and feelings will be very helpful for you as you move through the rest of the exercises in the book. You will be able to express what you are feeling and gain better understanding of yourself and your experiences.

If you are not familiar with a journaling practice you can begin one at any time. Some people have found it helpful to begin the practice of writing instead of journaling. A writing practice would be a daily routine where you sit and write about anything that comes to mind for a small period. The journaling practice would be you intentionally writing about a particular area such as how you are feeling; how you interpret a current or past experience or any other topic you would want to write about. The journaling process supports you in creating awareness of how you are feeling or of your perceptions. You can create a routine around writing if you schedule yourself 5 minutes during each day and just write about anything. The routine becomes around writing and it doesn't matter what you write about. The idea is to create the practice of writing and then when you do have something you do want to journal about, the practice or routine is already in place and supports the journaling process.

Chapter 2
The Games We Play That Get In Our Way

We play games all the time. Games entertain us and sometimes we do it just to have fun. We can play games while playing other games at the same time. We can play board games or card games with family and/or friends while laughing and playing at teasing one another. The combinations are as vast as we are individuals. The question becomes, "are the games helpful in some way"? Games can relieve stress while enjoying some time connecting with loved ones. They can help you adapt to some of life's challenges and be used as coping mechanisms. Games can support us and they also can distract us. Sometimes the games we play can get in our way. Games are played while we are in our roles we assume in life and masks we can wear in those roles. These roles can even be handed down to us from our earliest childhood experiences from our family members and we repeat these roles as adults in our lives. When the games or roles are not supporting us in a helpful way, then it becomes useful to create some awareness around what games or roles we are using in non helpful ways.

I had a friend who loved to play a "drama game." She could take the smallest situation and enlarge the details to enormous portions. I often found myself laughing with her on her exaggerations. As our friendship deepened, I also started to notice as soon as things calmed down around her, she began to search for new things with which to create more drama. Peace and calm were not familiar companions for my friend. I noticed it did take its toll on her own peace of mind at times. The drama game appeared to become a type of distraction for her where she could direct her focus instead of other places in her life which were trying to get her attention.

I had another friend who played the "busy game." She was always complaining how she never had enough time. I also saw her fill up any time that did become available with any activity that was readily available closest to her. These are games we play in our life to create distractions. As human beings we also are clever enough to play multiple games at the same time.

I became aware I played a "victim game." As I began to accept myself in more situations, I noticed a pattern or a repeating dynamic playing out in my relationships with others. I saw I played out a pattern of being a victim. I was a victim of the circumstance, others, and how I saw myself in general.

The belief pattern of being a victim was established early in my childhood and was very strong. I perceived situations or events as happening to me. I invested further in my belief I was a victim by validating it with others. If I complained to my friends, then I could count on them to feel sorry for me, my position as a victim was strengthened and I got to be right. See I am right, I am a victim.

The truth however, I was much more powerful in the creation of the situations around me. The truth of this was hidden by my desire to be right. As a victim I didn't have to take responsibility for all of my actions or choices that I made. I could place the blame on something or someone outside of myself and engage in being a victim.

In this perception, things were always going to happen to me. I could name, blame and feel sorry for myself while always having it be someone else's fault. I also became to feel pretty powerless, I saw things happening to me from the outside and I was at the mercy of what was happening.

As I moved more into accepting myself from within, I began to see the world was actually mirroring how I had felt about me in an outward reflection. The question came, "Did I want to be right, or did I want to see the truth"? It boiled down to a choice and I started to see that, choice is a powerful thing. We make choices all the time, but how often are we making choices from a conscious and aware state? When

I made the choice to face myself, I became aware that as I saw myself as a victim, so did the world and it reacted accordingly.

In order to accept myself as a victim, I needed to face myself, and see the game for what it was, just a game I was playing. I found it easier to realize I was not alone in this game. When I could see it for myself, I could start to see the game was played all around me. I started to understand we are only victims when we choose to believe we are. Yes bad things do happen. I speak from the voice of many experiences. Bad things happen yet those bad things are not who we are. We decide who we are with our own choices. I used that same power we all have in our choices by making the choice to accept myself. It all began with a choice.

Have you ever felt like something happened to you? Have you ever felt powerless in a situation? Have you ever felt like someone else wronged you and you wanted to get revenge? Have you ever called yourself a victim or said I am innocent in all of this? If you answered yes to just one of these questions, then you too have played the victim game. How much you have played this game in your life will be to the extent you see your life affected by it. If you have only played it a few times, then you will not see it as dramatically affecting you, as I did. If you did not answer yes, than you have just played a different game. You can insert any of the games we humans have played through the eons of time and replace "victim" with whatever game you chose to play. The dynamics will be the same. To accept yourself from whatever game you chose to play will require courage. The courage to face yourself, and then to accept yourself. It all starts with a choice.

I would suggest you create a safe space for yourself when you begin this exploration. The safe space could be fashioned through a quiet and peaceful environment in which to do this work. The safe space will be whatever you create and with whom you feel is appropriate to be with you. In later chapter 11, I offer suggestions for breathing exercises and relaxation techniques you might find helpful while doing this work. If you have trauma in your background and are concerned about the impact of this exercise, then I would suggest doing this work with a licensed health care professional. A professional will have the training to help guide you through the process. I would ask you to spend a moment here and feel into you and see what you feel is right for you and to follow your own guidance.

Exercises

As you did the previous exercises in Chapter 1, what patterns or dynamics did you see emerge? Did you find yourself playing out a role in your situations where you started to see yourself in? Example: I saw myself provoked in many situations and found myself reacting to another. This would be an example of a victim role. Start to create some awareness of key words such as, "it happened to me" or "it was their fault", or other words you have used that can indicate a role you were playing. Write out your role and how you have seen it play out in your life.

_____

_____

_____

_____

_____

_____

_____

_____

_____

_____

_____

To face this role completely will require to see it in all of its dimensions as it has played out in your life. I want to congratulate you so far, you have done so well, but a bit more is required. How has this role benefitted you? What was the motivation for you to continue to play this role? Example: I didn't have to take full responsibility for my choices and actions. I could blame another and feel better about myself. Please use your own words to describe how this role has helped you and try to find as many possible ways it has helped you.

_____

_____

_____

_____

_____

_____

_____

_____

_____

How has this role harmed you or gotten in your way? Example: I was often worried about what other people would try to do to me. I felt powerless in many circumstances and was at the mercy of what was happening around me. Please use your own words to describe how this role has blocked you from being who you really are.

_____

_____

_____

_____

_____

_____

_____

_____

I now will ask you to make a choice between the knowledge of how this role has helped you, and how it has not, and if you want to keep this role. There is no right or wrong answer, this is your decision and you know what is right for you. You can release the role the same way you started to accept yourself in chapter 1. It starts with a choice and then creating awareness around the fact you have been playing it. Again, be compassionate with yourself, you have played this role for many years and it will take time and practice to let go of the patterning. As you catch yourself in the role, try not to judge yourself for being in the role. Accept yourself in the role, congratulate yourself for becoming aware of it and make the choice to stop playing the role. I suggest you use the same exercises again in Chapter 1 to help you accept yourself playing the role as many times as you find appropriate.

_____

_____

_____

_____

_____

_____

_____

_____

_____

Once you have started this process, I would propose to you a new perception or way of seeing circumstances in your life. From the perspective where circumstances or events are happening to you, to a shift of circumstances or events that are bringing something for you. Every experience we have brings us something. Sometimes we like the "something", and sometimes we don't. I have found when I didn't like the "something", I was unable to see it was actually a gift. I will be the first to agree that sometimes these gifts come poorly wrapped with barbed and razor wire. However, once you get through the wire and open it up, there is gift and this circumstance has something to show you.

I found it helpful to shift the perspective from it was happening to me when I could start to look for what each experience was bringing to me. I could start to see patterns emerge where a certain theme would play out. I have found awareness is the first step and it was when I could see it, that I could make a choice of what I wanted to do with it. We have a choice to either use our experiences to empower us or to become disempowered, but we need the awareness first to make this choice. Every experience became my teacher and brought me exactly what I needed to learn more about me.

It is the shift in perception that provides the space in which you can let go of viewing yourself as victim and start to see yourself as the powerful creator you truly are. As I viewed myself as victim, so did the world and I had many experiences as a victim.

When I let go of the perception of a victim, I let go of having the experiences as a victim. I have witnessed that I create the world around me by how I feel and believe about myself and the world.

Chapter 3

Forgiveness

Buddha once said "**Holding onto anger is like drinking poison and expecting the other person to die**".

When we find ourselves in situations with others who have caused us grievances, we can find ourselves holding onto how we felt during these situations. We carry the past actions of others with us in a memory, as well as how we felt betrayed, hurt, or any other painful feelings. The memory becomes loaded with emotional attachment to how we felt at the time. The emotionally loaded memory can trigger many of the emotions we experienced at the time. We will be the ones who carry this load and reactivate it easily when we discuss it with others. We get to re-invest in a way of how we felt wronged, every time we bring those remembrances up to the surface. We also get to feel the pain each time we do this, and it is us who drank the poison. Freedom from this poison requires forgiveness. The forgiveness is not to set the other person free, but rather to set yourself free. The forgiveness of another is not to allow them a free pass from the choices or actions that was done; it is to allow you a free pass from staying bound to those choices or actions. The act of forgiveness releases you from carrying any of the emotional charges of the experience into current or future relationships. To forgive another can be one of the greatest gifts you give yourself. The question becomes, "do you want to feel wronged, or do you want to feel free"? It is a choice, and a powerful one.

Making mistakes is part of the experience as a human. We all have experienced making mistakes, as well as having mistakes made to us. This allows the idea that we do the best we can in each moment, and so does everyone else. Even when we consider we each are doing the best we can in each moment, painful and hurtful moments happen. Sometimes someone else's best, doesn't meet our own needs or expectations.

The other side of this experience is when we feel we have wronged another. When it is our own actions that have caused the grievances. The memory of such an event will carry the same emotional charge as when it was done to us. It is the same poison with the same person drinking it, you. Forgiving yourself will allow you the same freedom, and is just as powerful as forgiving another. The question becomes, "Do you want to feel guilt or shame, or do you want to feel free?". Can you allow yourself the freedom to accept you did the best you could in that situation, while considering all of the influences that were happening outside of you? It is a choice you can make and it is the same choice you made when you started to accept yourself. It is also a choice to not repeat the same experiences you have had before. It might be helpful to remind yourself you now carry the wisdom from all of the experiences you have had and now can use this wisdom at your discretion.

As I began the journey of forgiveness, I noticed it didn't happen magically in that moment. Instead more moments came until there was just forgiveness. It comes one step at a time, one declaration at a time, to forgive you or another.

Whenever I found myself repeating an old story of how I was wronged, I stopped myself and told myself it is an old story I no longer need. I used spoken declarations announcing "I forgive me" or another in the mirror.

I wrote out on paper declarations of forgiveness to me or another. I forgive me for everything. I forgive my life for everything. I forgive me for anything I think I did wrong. I forgive myself for ever thinking I did anything wrong. Forgiveness became the key to setting me free from being a victim.

Exercises

Who do you have to forgive? Spend a few moments reflecting on who you might be still holding a resentment or grievance against, and don't forget yourself. Write the names down below. You can begin the work of forgiveness at anytime and there is no right or wrong way to undergo it.

_____

_____

_____

_____

_____

_____

_____

_____

_____

_____

You can use the following affirmations or any others that feel right for you: I forgive _____, I forgive myself for any part I had in this co-creation, I forgive myself for believing I did anything wrong, I honor the insight this experience has brought me and release any resentments or grievances towards _____ or myself.

Useful tips

Use exercises in Chapter 1 for any situations where you find yourself experiencing any difficulty in accepting your actions. The acceptance of yourself will greatly assist you in forgiving yourself.

You may find it helpful to allow yourself to express how you felt about what happened. The expression of your feelings can be supportive in forgiving whoever you are trying to forgive. If you are unable to express this directly to the person, writing a letter to him/her can be therapeutic. You do not need to deliver the letter unless you feel it is appropriate, rather it is about you allowing yourself to express how you feel. Once you have allowed yourself to express it, you also will find it easier to release the burden you have been carrying.

The act of forgiveness helps to release you from replaying out thoughts of how you were wronged and the emotions that come with the thoughts. The memory of how you were wronged can still be present but it will be a memory of the event without the emotional charge or attachment. Forgiveness can also allow compassion in the understanding the other person did do they best she/he was able to, even in the action of wronging you.

I found it helpful to write declarations of forgiveness and post them on the mirror or near my computer. I wrote the declarations stating what I was forgiving. Use whatever words feel right for you. You are creating an intention more powerful than the words you choose to write it out with.

Imagine an average pencil you used during your childhood education experiences. It is long, yellow, has a metal band, and an eraser. Although different manufacturers produce pencils, they generally use the same design in producing pencils. They seem to have gone to quite a bit of trouble to include the eraser through binding it in the metal band and is an important part of the design. Pencil manufacturers seem to assume we are going to make a mistake while using the pencil and need the eraser. Making mistakes is the place we can glean insight from our experiences and recognizing it is just part of the learning process allows us to forgive ourselves and others just a little easier. As long as we are judging ourselves or others for making mistakes, we can focus on what we or they have done wrong instead of what we have learned.

I also found it helpful to find one thing I appreciated about the person I was forgiving. Often when we focus on how wronged we were that becomes central in our awareness. When we allow appreciation or gratitude into our vision at the same time, it can allow the perception to shift a little and become easier to allow forgiveness in as well.

Chapter 4
What Do You Want?

We make choices from the first moment we awake to the last moment we fall asleep. One of the first choices we make when we first awaken is what we are going to place our attention on. What type of day is it going to be, what do we have to get done, where do we have to be and when? We are constantly making choices and just as often we make those choices by default. We often can make a choice quickly throughout the day by assessing what we want and then are unaware we are doing because it is happening so fast. We also are unaware how many choices we dismiss in this process because at first glance in this fast process, it doesn't look like a viable alternative. How many choices have you already made today? So much of what happens in our lives is a choice, and a choice we make, regardless if we make that choice with awareness or not. I found for myself, I made many choices by default because I did not see I was making a choice. I had a belief system, or a way I was seeing myself in the world, that was influencing what I believed about the world. What I believed directly influenced what I thought I could choose and what I could not. When I did not see the choices I actually was making, I had no power over the choices I was making. The power comes from the ability to see it is a choice and to make a choice from a place of what is actually wanted.

I found I had many beliefs around what someone else had told me was right or wrong and this was directly affecting what choices I was making. I decided to then throw away everyone else's versions of what was right for me and to start guiding myself in what I wanted. It started with a question I asked myself, "What do I want?" This is a great time to ask yourself this same thing. What I wanted transformed into a compass that guided my choices. The compass did require authenticity and that meant I needed to see all the potentials of what my choice was and if I still wanted it after I saw the potentials.

When you ask yourself what you want, you start to create awareness. The awareness arrives first in what you desire, and then how the choice can manifest in your life. The next step is to look at all the potentials of that choice in how it can manifest in positive and negative ways in your life. Once you create the awareness of those potentials, ask if those potentials are what you want. If the potentials of that choice are based in what you want, then you have selected the choice you want. If they are not, then choose again. The great thing about choices, when there is one available, there is always more available as well. When I looked closer at situations when I thought I didn't have a choice, I began to see it was not my choices that were limited but rather my perspective around the choices that had the limitations. The limitation of the perspective of our choices is what can hold us back and this is the very place you want to use as wide angle of a lens as you can.

Look at all the potentials around your choice, look for every outcome to create as much awareness around it as you can. The awareness brings the gift of clarity, the clarity to choose what you want with discrimination. I found as I created the awareness around my choice that I also saw more choices available to me and they were often worthy of consideration.

Exercises

Ask yourself, "What do I want?" You can let this question flow to any part of your life. Initially it might be easier to integrate this question by starting with something smaller and start to build confidence in using this formula.

_____

_____

_____

_____

_____

_____

_____

Begin to look at all the possible outcomes of what this choice can bring into your life. By creating awareness around all the potentials of your choice, you create the awareness of whether you really do want this choice. First, list all the positive potentials you can see from this choice and then ask, "do I want these potentials?"

_____

_____

_____

_____

_____

_____

_____

_____

_____

List all the negative potentials, or outcomes that could adversely affect you from this choice. This is an important step in creating the awareness of how your choice can manifest in your life and is important to take your time. Ask yourself, "do I want these potentials?"

_____

_____

_____

_____

_____

_____

_____

Once you have created the awareness of your choice by looking at the potentials, you then can make the decision if you still want the choice. If you do still want the choice then it will be helpful to begin an action plan of what steps are necessary to begin implementing this choice. You can begin by asking yourself what are some action steps you need to begin taking to start moving in this direction, what can you do to support yourself more in these steps, and what resources do you need to do this? It is in asking what you want that allows you to create a compass. The compass becomes a tool you use in your very own guidance system that is already waiting for you to tap into. This tool will also require you to use it with discernment and wisdom. You already have this wisdom and discernment as well, and you access it by creating the awareness around what potentials or outcomes are possible and then using your guidance system of what you want to create the clarity of what decisions you want to make. You are your own best source of guidance and it is waiting for you within.

As you start to create some confidence in choosing what you want with awareness, you also will find it useful to start creating some awareness around how many choices you have made that you are not aware of. The awareness of what choices have been made through default will be useful if they are done without judging yourself for it.

It is important to keep the self acceptance integrating into all parts of you and will be useful here as well. Whatever decisions you have made without awareness were done when you were doing the best you could and it is good enough. If you question this at all, go back and review all of the outside and inside influences that were happening around you when you made those decisions and lower whatever bar of expectation you had for yourself to a more reasonable level.

Creating the awareness of when in the past you have made decisions without being conscious of them will help you in becoming more aware of them as they arrive in your situations now or in the future. This experience has brought you the gift of clarity and awareness and you now can use it in all future experiences and start to create the awareness around your decisions and start choosing what you do want. These patterns also have been running in the background for a long time and you are familiar with them. It will take practice and compassion with yourself while you are learning and changing the patterns. If you do catch yourself making choices without awareness, congratulate yourself for creating the awareness you are. It is the awareness of what we are doing that is the first and most important step. It is only when we can see it, can we choose to do anything about it.

The understandings of how to do this work came through my own inner knowingness but there is also a therapy called "Reality Therapy" which is somewhat similar and can provide additional resources if you choose to do independent research on the therapy.

Chapter 5
Don't Take What Doesn't Belong To You

In Chapter 1, I wrote about how we live in a world of relationships. We are all interconnected and interacting on varying levels daily. Each person encountered is affected by these relationships and interacts with others through how she/he perceives and thinks about whom they are in contact with, how they feel about themselves and what is happening outside of them. Whatever we express through speech or actions, will reflect our beliefs, perspectives, our relationship with the world and how we feel within about who we are. We reflect who we are through what we express in each moment. How another person perceives and responds to those expressions reflects what is within her/himself. We each are a mirror for ourselves and reflect ourselves back continuously.

Sometimes the boundaries of ownership can be crossed and we take what doesn't belong to us. If someone behaves inconsiderately, insults or criticizes us, we can take it in and personalize it. The truth is that it belongs to who expressed it and it is a choice of each individual if they want to own it too. The resulting expression is an opinion, and it may or may not be true for you as well. I found that as I took responsibility for my own choices and actions, I also began to become aware of when I was taking responsibility for what was not mine. I started to understand when I reacted to another's expression that it actually was reflecting a belief, or a perspective within me that was surfacing for me to make a choice if I still wanted to keep it. I started to pay attention to these reactions and was grateful to be able to see them for what they really were. Many times I found that when I applied the "test of truth" to them, they were not true. The "test of truth" is simply looking for the evidence if it is true or not. If it is not true and you have taken ownership of another's expression, then you are giving yourself a gift of awareness that you now can use discernment and make a choice with. Is it yours or are you taking what does not belong to you? If you have accepted another's truth and it is not your truth, you can easily give it back by simply making the choice within you. I found it empowering to simply recognize when it is not mine and choose to not accept it as mine.

Try placing a folder or some other object against your body and close to your heart. How does it feel when it is this close to you? Try to describe the physical attributes of it. If it is a folder, try to describe any papers that are inside of the folder. As long as you have not memorized the object, you would have difficulty discerning the physical attributes because you cannot see it clearly when it is held close to you. You can feel it strongly but do not see it clearly. Now take the object and hold it at arm's length. You will be able to see it more objectively and will feel it through your fingertips but the feeling will not be as strong. If it is a folder you now can open it up and see what is inside. Try to use this construct with situations that happen around you. Take the situation or experience out of your heart where you feel it more strongly and hold it away from you where you can see it more clearly and objectively.

This allows the situation or experience to be given "the light of day" or be brought more objectively into your awareness. Give it the "test of truth", and ask "does this really belong to me or is it an expression of someone else?"

I found it empowering to see the reaction as an invitation and remove all judgment around the reaction as right or wrong. I looked within for the insight that could show me what the reaction was bringing me to see. What I found was I was reacting to another's expression because it had triggered a belief or perspective within me that was operating below my aware and conscious state. The reaction provided the opportunity to look a little deeper and see it for what it was, instead of what it was pretending to be. The more awareness I could create about myself, helped me to decide what I wanted to keep and what was no longer true for me.

Exercises

Write about a situation where you felt criticized or hurt by another's comments.

_____

_____

_____

_____

_____

_____

_____

_____

_____

What hurt you the most about this situation? "Give it the light of day." Look for keywords such as "they made me feel like" and remind yourself you are responsible for how you feel, it is your choice and no one else can make you feel anything. Try to see an indication which can show a belief or perspective within you that was triggered by this experience.

_____

_____

_____

_____

_____

_____

_____

_____

_____

_____

Give the comments or situation the "test of truth." What evidence or facts are present which provide this as true? If it is not true, then this is not about you. This is about the person who made the comments or who is involved in the situation, and it belongs to them. This is the time to make a choice, do you still want this or do you want to give it back to them by recognizing it is not yours? I found it useful to create an image of handing back whatever was not mine to the person it belonged to in my mind. I said the words in my mind "you can have this back, it is not mine and I don't want it."

It is the process of creating awareness of when something is pretending to be something it is not that allows you to "Give it the light of day", and then apply "Test of Truth", and empower you to decide what is yours, and what is not.

As I explored deeper into what was not mine, I began to understand the effects of sympathy, empathy, and compassion. Sympathy could be defined as feeling for someone, while empathy would be feeling with someone. Compassion is not feeling for anyone else but holding the understanding of what someone else's experience is. Pretend you have a close friend whom you care very much for. She is eating at restaurant with you and she begins to not feel very well and becomes concerned it is the food she has just eaten. In a place of sympathy, you would eat some of the food on her plate to test it out and show her you care. You now are also fully experiencing her nausea and you both are miserable because of it. In empathy, your stomach began hurting as you listened to her complaints and neither of are doing well now. In compassion, you would understand your friend's misery and begin asking her if she wants to go to urgent care, or buy some charcoal to help remove the toxins from her body. In compassion you do not have the emotional reactivity you would in either sympathy or empathy but rather stand in your empowerment and can see and support her from a much more objective and clear place. I also have experienced sympathy and empathy as taking what was not mine when I walked into another's experience and had been far more supportive and helpful when I remained in compassion.

Although these techniques are different, there is a therapy called "Narrative Therapy" which is close enough to offer you an additional resource if you should choose to research it.

Chapter 6
Going Within

Within each of us lies an internal guidance system where we can tap into our own inner wisdom. This is an ever flowing system, operates 24 hours a day, 7 days a week and comes already installed. You do not need to know how to read any particular code, or know a particular language to use it, but it does require some listening. This system also requires some inquiries by you to begin to access it. I first became aware of my own inner guidance when I began making inquiries into myself about how to stay true to my own authenticity. Yes that will be the other catch to this system, it requires you to be authentic with you.

Authenticity allows one to interact within one's world and relationships within that world from a place of empowerment where the person remains true and honest unto one's self. The person who utilizes authenticity is not influenced to act or react towards others from an expectation of what or how she/he should be but rather how he/she chooses to be. This allows the person to decide for her/himself what is of value or meaningful to her/him rather than accepting someone else's definition. Being authentic means I am not always going to agree with everyone or fit into every situation. Sometimes the price of remaining authentic means "you cannot go along to just get along" and standing in your truth sometimes can be a lonely spot to be in. I have not been authentic at times when I was more interested in fitting into a situation with other people rather than being in the truth of who I am. I now realize when this happens and I remind myself it is more important that I feel I am in my truth than meeting someone else's expectation of me. Our roles, defense mechanisms, expectations, and wanting to fit in often can influence us in remaining in authenticity. The more awareness we can create around what roles we are playing, how we protect ourselves, the expectations others have for us, and accepting ourselves as is, will allow us to make more conscious choices of what we want. It is from this place you can access your internal wisdom.

Making the inquiry of "what is my intention or motivation in this action" will allow one to create more awareness of what one is doing, what identity one is in and what one actually wants in each situation. To really access your guidance system, you must be willing to be honest with yourself and use courage to face yourself. When I first began making these inquiries into my actions I didn't always like the answer I got nor did I want to see myself from an angle I normally would judge as inappropriate. I began to learn how to detach from assigning any meanings or values to my discoveries or insights and moved into a role of just observing. As I observed what my true intentions or motivations were in each particular situation, I created the awareness to see it as it is and then began to decide for myself what I really wanted in that situation. Sometimes when I could see what I really was trying to do in a particular action, I realized I didn't really want to continue to pursue it and I let go.

My own internal wisdom taught me it is not the thing (an object or situation) which trips us up, but rather what meaning we have put around the thing. If I told someone "I love apples", the person's perception of what an apple was to her/him would allow a person to apply a value of what my statement meant to her/him. The perception would be based on previous experiences with apples, meanings and values attached to apples.

These are the perceptions around the thing, all the judgments and meanings we attach to issues, people, situations, and objects which is subjective to each of us and only true when we believe it is. Regardless of how each of us perceives the apple and applies different values to it, in the end it is just an apple or the thing. We also can limit ourselves with our own definitions. As soon as we define a thing, we have limited it with that definition of what it is. The thing can still be more but we do not see it past our own definition. We only see the thing from our subjective familiarity even though it may be quite different to others. When we can begin to let go of what is around the thing, and allow the thing to be what it is, we can let go of our attachments or meanings which may no longer be true for us.

What is true? It is what we believe and we need to remember it is only one perception. When we open ourselves up to the idea there is more than one perception, we can then decide which ones do we want to consciously choose? What do I want, how do I choose to see this, is this empowering me or disempowering me, what is my intention? These were some of the inquiries I used to access my own inner wisdom and then of course I had to be willing to listen. What is to be gained by tapping into your own wisdom? You. You gain you and begin to create a relationship with yourself in which you become "the you" you choose to be. It was in this place I began to learn how to trust myself. I started feeling into things instead of just watching it with my eyes. I started to see if it was resonating with me or not. You know the feeling in your gut, the feel of a room when you first walk in, or any other sensory perceptions we can too easily ignore? How often were you right when you first felt into something? I found I was already doing it but had learned to ignore it and not use my intuition. It was as simple as recognizing it was already there for me and then begin to practice using it.

Exercises

What is authenticity? Spend a few moments and reflect how do you define authenticity?

_____

_____

_____

_____

_____

_____

_____

_____

_____

Why would you want to be more authentic and what can it bring you that is helpful?

_____
_____
_____
_____
_____
_____
_____

How have you been inauthentic in your life?

_____
_____
_____
_____
_____
_____
_____

What has gotten in your way of being authentic? What roles are you playing in your life and how are those roles affected by others expectations of you?

_____
_____
_____
_____
_____
_____
_____

What can authenticity bring you that could be uncomfortable?

_____

_____

_____

_____

_____

_____

How can you be more authentic in your life? What changes can you make in your life now to bring in more authenticity?

_____

_____

_____

_____

_____

_____

_____

Reflect back on the most recent experience you can think of when you were interacting with another. What was your intention or motivation in that interaction? What did you want to achieve? Is the motivation what you really want now or can you adjust your motivation to be more in alignment with who you are? Begin using this inquiry with yourself as much as you can, in as many experiences you have.

_____

_____

_____

_____

_____

_____

The understandings of how to do this work came through my own inner knowingness and had already been using this myself and then with clients as I attended graduate school to become a clinical social worker and a mental health counselor. As I moved further along in my course studies I began to be exposed to various theories and you will have already found some of them referenced in previous chapters. Each time I began to learn some of the theories I became stunned and astonished how similar they were to what I was already doing. I then began to understand just how powerful inner wisdom can be and how well it can serve each and every one of us. Each of the theories I mention will not be the same as I use them, my own inner wisdom accessed a different angle or approach but they are close enough to mention. In this chapter you may choose to do some independent research into "Existentialism" and find some more additional resources.

Where does this higher wisdom come from? It has been known by many names such as soul, spirit, higher self, and all that I am. I found I could access more of my own inner wisdom through the use of inquiries. I began asking myself more questions that would allow me to access more of me from a larger perspective. How would I understand this from all that I am? I used any inquiries in any form about anything in my life and my requirement was to allow myself some quiet and still moments that invited the answers to be heard. I began feeling into as much as I could around me and became aware I did indeed have much more of an intuitive sense available to me than I had been aware of before. I invited more of me into my focus here.

Chapter 7
Calling You Home

Words by Kevyn Aucoin: **"Today I choose life. Every morning when I wake up I can choose joy, happiness, negativity, pain…. To feel the freedom that comes from being able to continue to make mistakes and choices-today I choose to feel life, not to deny my humanity, but to embrace it".**

We often can accept feeling joy or bliss easily but how easily can we accept feeling negativity, anger or even pain? My inner wisdom guided me to feel what I feel and yet feeling bad did not feel good and I had the pattern of pushing away the feelings I didn't like. If someone rejects you, you feel the rejection, and you can push away the feeling of being rejected because it is painful. Yet the feeling you just pushed away was just as much a part of you as any other feeling you have. You now have rejected yourself and I found the most damage was done, not by the other person rejecting me, but by me rejecting me by pushing away what I was feeling. Our feelings bring understanding to us in how we perceive what is happening around us. When we push part of us away, we splinter the part we didn't want. This part of us does not leave but continues to hang around and join layers of other parts we have pushed away previously. The old adage "The straw that broke the camel's back" speaks directly to this. Was it the one straw that broke the camel or was it layers upon layers of straw that became the burden the camel could no longer carry?

Have you ever experienced an emotional reaction that managed to be blown out of proportion to what was actually happening? Chances are, you too have experienced the effect from layering feelings you have pushed away and the addition of one more, tipped the scale and brought on the reaction. We can bury or push away all the feelings we do not like or want but in the end they always find a way to come home to us.

To feel what you feel requires feeling all feelings, regardless of how you have judged or perceived them. I found it useful to become an observer of the feelings and detach from applying any value or meaning to the feeling other than what it was trying to show me. I detached as well from assigning any blame or fault to me or anyone else and reminded myself I was doing the best I could and so was everyone else. The emotional states of anger, sadness, happiness, excitement, and many others are mental feelings produced by thoughts, beliefs and perceptions of the mind that also can trigger physical responses in the body. They are only as real as we believe them to be. This can be a challenging concept to recognize when one is caught in the throes of their experience but also can be helpful to shift a strong emotional response when challenged that it is only as real as is the belief in it.

I also found it helpful to use deep breathing through any challenging feelings that presented. The deep breath through the nose all the way to the belly and out the mouth allowed me to place focus on the breathing while maintaining my attention on the feeling.

As I began to allow feelings happening in the present experiences, I began to feel my emotional load lighten as the feelings were allowed to integrate into me and be released once they were able to show me what they wanted me to see.

As I integrated and released present time feelings, older feelings I pushed away previously began coming back home too. I found this happened sometimes spontaneously or when a memory or event triggered the feelings back into present time. I used the deep breath to work through the feeling and sometimes used the well known mantra "this too shall pass" as I needed to help with the integration and release. I stayed as much as I could in the observer role and accepted it as it was. I found this sometimes to be a bit of a challenge. All too often these feelings were not acceptable, they didn't feel good, and often felt contrary to who I was. How do I accept the unacceptable? I accepted it from there, as it was, and as uncomfortable. I found acceptance was not about being acceptable, acceptance was accepting it as it is and in any form it takes. The shift in my perception that allowed me to accept anything as it was without first transmuting it into an acceptable form assisted me greatly in finding acceptance of all that is. It does indeed pass and I found as I kept the breath moving, exhaling and immediately beginning the inhale after the exhale, I could feel it start to break up and finally release.

I do want to place a disclaimer where I inform you this is another portion of the book you need to feel into you. Is it resonating for you to begin this work or would you be more comfortable working with a licensed mental health professional? You are your own best guide and feel into what you feel is best for you. If you choose to work with a licensed mental health professional simply let them know what you want to work on and you can find one who can work with you on this. The understandings of how to do this work came through my own inner knowingness but there is also a therapy called "Mindfulness" which is similar and can produce the same results. Look for someone who is trained to use this theoretical approach. You can also do some independent research into "Mindfulness" and use as additional resources.

I also began to do some work with myself first and then with clients with past traumatic episodes. As we go back into the time and place where the trauma happened we have the opportunity to do something very powerful. We can show ourselves to be the one who made it to the other side of the experience. If you return to when you were originally in the experience, all of the emotional reactivity from the experience can be all that is in your focus. You may not see you are on the other side of the experience, the one which made it through. However when you return to the older version of you, you can show the stuck, trapped part of you in the trauma you can make it through, you are here afterwards and looking to make peace with it. Even more important, you are willing to accept it exactly as it is, you are not trying to change it, or push it away.

I have often wondered if part of us became trapped because as we push away the experience or the feelings because it hurts too much we inadvertently push part of ourselves who experienced it too. We don't want to feel that part of ourselves which is hurting, that is in pain and we push that part away and reject it. It can be the same mechanism of the experience in the pain and hurt we feel at the time and do not feel safe, wanted or accepted outside of ourselves, and then we in turn push us away from within.

I found for me this was the most traumatic part of the experience, when I pushed myself away because I didn't want to feel or experience the pain I was in. In chapter 3 I asked if you could find one thing you could appreciate about the person you were trying to forgive to help shift the perception in forgiveness. I ask you to search here as well for one thing you can appreciate about the experience to help shift it as well. Is it possible this experience had a quality or portion that was about love or appreciation? If you can find it, use it. I found finding something about the experience which was based in love or something to appreciate about it to be very useful in shifting my own perceptions.

I found journaling about my experiences, my feelings, and my interpretation of all of it to be helpful in assisting me in becoming aware of what I was feeling. I also used the sensations in my body to help me identify feelings. I found I manifested how I perceived the world around me through my body. When I was happy I felt my heart area open widely and felt free and light. When I was sad I could feel it constricted and tight. I began paying attention to how I was feeling in my body and would check in with myself each hour that passed. As I checked in with me I began noticing that my body was communicating with me. I also noticed patterns in how I expressed my emotions in my body. When I was unsure or anxious in a situation my stomach would hurt. I began using the hourly check in as a way to monitor how I was feeling. When I felt something in my body I also began inquiring how I was perceiving whatever was around me. I used the deep breath work and challenged any perceptions with the "test of truth" that were pretending to be something they were not.

Exercises

What sensations do you feel in your body now? Can you think of a time your stomach hurt, throat was constricted and had trouble talking, or your heart area felt tight? What was happening in your environment? How did you perceive it? Did you feel safe or the need to protect yourself?

_____

_____

_____

_____

_____

_____

_____

_____

_____

_____

Start tracking the sensations you feel in your body and inquire into what your body is trying to tell you. I found it helpful to journal about what I felt that day, and what discoveries I found when I checked in with myself each hour. If you find monitoring your body each hour too difficult, find an amount of time for each check in that is appropriate for you. The most impactful part of this exercise is to increase your awareness of what you are feeling in your body and what it wants to tell you about how you perceive your world. The deep breath also will allow you to be in the feeling, integrate it and then release it. I often will have clients begin blowing bubbles when I first teach them deep breath work. In order to blow bubbles, you must breathe deeply first and helps to get deep breath moving as well as just being fun.

What feelings or emotions have you been pushing away or not wanting to see? Reflect on the question for a moment and bring one of the feelings or emotions out. If you cannot raise one to the surface, try to think of an experience which you found troubling. As you start to feel the emotion begin the deep breath and keep the breath going until the emotion starts to break up and release. Remain an observer as much as you can through this experience and stand on the side of it as it happens and simply watch what it is expressing. Keep breathing and after you do feel it release, write about your experience here.

_____

_____

_____

_____

_____

_____

_____

_____

_____

_____

As you move through your day try to watch for any emotions or feelings you might have. Breathe through the emotion and remain an observer as much as you can until it releases. Keep journaling about all the emotions and feelings you are allowing to come home and be released. I found it very encouraging and motivating to read my journal later and show myself I really could feel what I feel.

Chapter 8

Fear

"Let me not pray to be sheltered from dangers, but to be fearless in facing them. Let me not beg for the stilling of my pain, but for the heart to conquer it." ~ Rabindranath Tagore

Fear is a feeling we all have felt at various times in our lives, and can be the most frightening of all of our emotional states. The fear that can paralyze you and consume any feeling of power you might have once owned. Can you face such a thing? What about anxiety? The fear that is projected in the future about what might happen? Joe R. Wilner LMLP granted me permission to cite his article "How to break your worry habit and overcome anxiety" published in Psych Central. In Joe's article he talks about things we can worry about will not actually happen 90% of the time and the 10% of the time the things we worry about are valid and yet solutions are often available for these concerns. If what we can worry about is not valid concerns that can actually happen 90% of the time, why are we worrying or projecting our fears into the future? Dr. Yvonne Hall gave the best explanation I have heard thus far. She said it was our ancestors who could survive if they reacted to fear and ran away from a predator trying to eat them. If you didn't run away then you probably would not survive and be able to reproduce offspring. The ones who could become fearful survived and became our ancestors. She described this as we are genetically predisposed to have fear and anxiety. She also stated anxiety was simply a form of energy and the more you could use the energy from your anxiety to perform an activity you wanted to do, the better you were able to burn that energy off.

I found when I allowed the fear or worry to remain in my mind, I could chase my tail in my mind all day and really scare myself. I gave the fear or worry the "light of day" and wrote it out on paper where I could see it more objectively and then apply "the test of truth" to it and look for evidence to see if it was true or not. I often found exactly what Joe described in his article, the fear or worry was not valid and highly likely it was not even going to happen. If I kept the fear or worry in my head though, I could convince myself it was very likely and give myself quite the scare. I also found it helpful to remind myself when I felt fear that it was just an emotional state, like anger, sadness, or any other emotion the mind could experience.

Is this true of all fears? Not for me and I did find some deeply embedded fears that simply bringing them out into the open was not enough to dispel their ability to really frighten me. I found some fears were deeply entrenched enough into my subconscious that it took deeper work to allow them to release. I used the same technique I did with integrating and releasing feelings and breathed my way through the fear. I would allow the fear to emerge and breathe right into it and with enough breath work; I found it too began to release. I found fear was but an aspect within the mind, the shadow that could fall upon me that was actually trying to protect me. I have a mind but I am not my mind, I am something much more and so are you. I am consciousness that uses the mind as a tool. The mind tries to interpret the world from a linear lens that often brings distortions to what we can think of as our reality. Fear is one of these distortions the mind interprets as real. It often can be an illusion, pretending to be something it is not but it also can be a very real illusion that can frighten us to our very core.

I found it helpful to create as much clarity as I could around the fear I was feeling, asking it what it wanted me to know, thank it for trying to protect me, look directly into the fear, look for any truth, validate if it was true or not, and then choose to release it. I found thanking my mind for showing me the fear an important dynamic which allowed me to embrace the fear instead of trying to push it away or resist it. Sometimes the fear was valid and was protecting me from something which could harm me and sometimes it was not valid but attempting to protect me all the same. I did not find it helpful to push it away or hide it and this only allowed the fear to be out of my sight but not gone and was effecting me without my awareness of it. It also could be layered among other fears I had pushed away exactly the same way I had pushed feelings from me. The layering of fears or other feelings allowed them to be more potent in their ability to affect me. I found every shadow aspect was serving a purpose and was not happening to me but rather bringing something for me. I had not been comfortable with my own shadow aspects of fear, doubt, regret, shame, guilt, and grievances and had been pushing part of myself away. Each of these aspects was trying to communicate how I was experiencing my world and yet I had not wanted to listen.

I find every emotion, and every reaction is my friend trying to communicate to me how I am perceiving my world. I judged these friends as wrong, working against me and not helpful. I can see now they have been faithful friends and are willing to do their job unconditionally. They stayed with me, kept trying to communicate with me regardless of how many times I pushed them away because I was uncomfortable with how they felt. Our feelings can be like the friend who wore a polka dotted shirt with striped pants. You tell her "this is not how we present ourselves out in the world. If others see me with you they might think we are the same. You are not acting nicely and you have to leave." The feeling, as your friend, is what it is, if it is sad, it becomes sadder to your response. If it is angry, it becomes angrier. If it is guilt, it feels more guilt, and if it is fear, it becomes more fearful. Our emotions communicate to us through what they are. Sadness communicates as sad, happy communicates as happy, and fear communicates as fear. They are what they are and communicate to us through what they are. With some of the emotions such as sadness or especially fear, physical sensations in the body can also be felt as very uncomfortable. Even though we may not like the way they communicate or how they feel in the body, they are trying to do their job. From this perception fear is actually a friend and not the foe it has the reputation as.

When these friends can be accepted as they are and what they bring, the perception of the shadow becomes the light and shifts into gratitude. I find every experience is perfection and bringing me exactly what I need to gain more clarity and understanding of me. This is the place you can walk openly and willingly into all your experiences knowing it is bringing you exactly what you need. When you can call all these parts and aspects of you home in acceptance, you step into your own mastery of yourself.

Whenever I am around heights I feel uncomfortable sensations in my body. I become dizzy, disoriented, my stomach jumps into my chest, trouble breathing, and I feel terror in my heart. I had this experience while driving on some mountain roads with my daughter as we drove to an area that had some cliff edges. I could immediately feel the physical sensations begin. I began talking to my fear. I validated the appearance of danger to my fear. "Yes, this does look like a pretty sharp cliff". I thanked my fear, "thank you fear, I am grateful you are trying to keep me safe." I also told my fear although it appeared to be a dangerous spot on the road, I was driving slow enough and had full control of the vehicle. Immediately the sensations within my body disappeared. I drove about 100 more yards and I began to feel the sensations again. I went through the same process with the fear through talking to it and then felt it leave. I found I needed to do the talk with my fear a total of 4 times during the drive through the mountains. I understood my fear just wanted to protect me and when I could validate it, thank it, and then determine I was actually ok, the fear listened to me as well.

Exercises

What fears do you have? Take some time and begin to write about what you are fearful of? Take as much time as you need and you may find it more comfortable to only write about one fear a day and spread this exercise out over as much time as you need.

_____

_____

_____

_____

_____

_____

_____

What is this fear trying to protect you and keep you safe from?

_____

_____

_____

_____

_____

_____

_____

_____

Is this a real danger or is it simply perceived as danger? If it is only a perception of danger and not a real threat, thank your fear for doing its job and validate the perception as not a real threat. You also can use this technique with any of your emotions and the result will be the same. If you do not know what the emotion is trying to communicate to you then ask it and allow a still moment for the answer to flow to you.

Where is your attention focused on? Are you in the present moment or have you slipped into the past or the future. Worry or anxiety often is fear projected into the future. The past is the past and you can do nothing helpful with it other than accepting it as it was. The future has not happened and only contains the potentials of what might be. It is a probability that does not hold any concrete validity to it until it happens in that now moment. If you catch yourself worrying about an event that might happen, remind yourself it might, but has not actually happened. Ask yourself how likely is this really going to happen? Are there any precautions I can take now to assist me with it? Bring yourself back to your present time as much as you can. I found it helpful to notice what was in my environment and start taking stock of what was there to help bring my focus more into the present moment when I caught myself in the past or the future. You also can use your 5 senses in any way and the focus on your sensory experience will bring you back into present time. I also found it very helpful to begin becoming very picky about what I was placing my focus on as I became aware how greatly that focus affected how I felt in that moment.

Chapter 9

Letting Go

How many times do we still hang onto items we no longer need, or really want but keep them around because they are familiar to us? What if some of these items were not only no longer useful to you, but were actually hindering you? What about control, the expression of us that has been labeled as bad and manipulative? Control seems to have gotten a bad reputation along the way but is actually a helpful mechanism in how it is used. How much control we feel we have within our experience and over ourselves can help us feel safe. I noticed a pattern within me when I reached for control around me, and it was to find security. I didn't actually have control over much that I was trying to reach but the illusion allowed me to feel less powerless. I also became frustrated when what I was trying to control was not allowing me to control it. I started to see it was my perception of control that was hindering me. The control I thought I had within my world. I saw control was a necessary expression of me when I was controlling what was mine to control. I found it is how I choose to express what was mine to control and not much else. I began to find I had control over two things, choice and perception, and that happened when I was aware of them. When I tried to control what was not mine, which were others or outcomes, then I ran into resistance. When I let go of trying to control the rest, I found peace.

As you do the work in the previous chapters hopefully you have begun to discover old beliefs about you, your roles, perceptions, and your relationship with the world you actually never chose yourself but was handed down to you by your family of origin, your peer group, and the world around you. We often are not aware how these beliefs are affecting us until we can create awareness around them. This is the place I have attempted to bring you to, awareness. The next step is to determine do you still want them or do you want to pick out your own beliefs and perceptions? I found the easiest way for me to release was to just let go, surrender, and choose what I did want. This is the place of no resistance, no pushing, or shoving. I experienced I first needed to become aware of it, choose if I still wanted it or choose what I did want, and then let go. I also found some of the old beliefs or perceptions had some sticking power and would come back up when it was triggered. I kept my awareness as much as I could when it would present and let go and surrender. If I reacted to the belief, tried to argue with it, or convince it was wrong I found it stuck harder. The emotional reaction gave it sticking power. It was when I could observe it without getting stuck in it that I found the ability to let it go.

What does letting go and surrendering bring? Initially letting go and surrendering was very difficult for me. From my earliest memories I was taught to take care of myself and ask no one for anything. This was how I survived and the belief I should do it myself was deeply ingrained. My inner knowingness however was guiding me to surrender and let go. I decided to trust me. I had put my trust in many things outside of me and often experienced disappointment, and at that point thought why not give me a try? I have never been disappointed in my decision since.

As I began to practice letting go and surrendering, I discovered it allowed the space for me to align into whatever was happening. It allowed the part of me here that does not understand, does not know how to release something, or do something to access the whole of me that does. It was never about me giving my power away, it was about me accessing the power I do have.

I surrendered to me, to my higher self, or my soul. I would guide you to surrender to whatever you are most comfortable surrendering to. It can be your higher power, god, your higher self or whatever is appropriate for you, the result will be the same. Each surrender experience has been a little different. Sometimes the help arrives or the understanding comes in on how to do whatever it is I am trying to do. Sometimes it happens instantly and whatever barrier is there is removed and sometimes it takes a little longer. The surrender allowed me to get out of the way and allow the space for something else and each one was unique to that particular situation. It has brought a synchronicity to my life I have never known before.

Letting go is letting go of your control and grasp on it. Place your hand in a fist and tighten it. Now release the fist and let go. You can use this image in your mind or use your hand to form a fist and let go on a belief, a perception, a situation, or anything else you need. If you use your hand then imagine putting whatever you are trying to let go of in your fist and then open your hand and let go. You can do the same thing in your mind by imagining a fist in your mind, placing what you want to let go of in the fist, and then open the fist up and let go. I let go in my mind where I feel the point of my consciousness fixed and let go. If none of these suggestions work for you then speak the words, "I release, and I let go." By letting go, you stop the resistance to what you are feeling or thinking about what is happening.

I also want to add some clarification of how I am defining resistance. If you start to rub your two hands together you will notice it will create friction and your hands will start to heat up. You have a barrier of skin between both hands that do not allow your hands to merge with one another. This is the action that happens with your perceptions or beliefs when you come in contact with something that is not congruent, in alignment or able to merge with you. This also can happen within you when you have two different beliefs that are polar opposites of each other. An example of this could be when you believe you should have something and at the same time you do not believe you are worthy. The two beliefs butt heads against each other and cause resistance or conflict. This resistance can happen within and can happen outside of you. If you find yourself judging something as bad or wrong then you can become aware you just hit some resistance to your own belief. It is not wrong and it is not right. The question becomes is it helpful and do you still want it? I found whenever I was in a place of resistance, letting go was the easiest way for me to shift my perception of it and find peace. I also found it helpful to not go into my mind and try to define it. The action of letting go was enough to shift the perception and then I placed my attention on something I did want to focus on.

To begin this new practice you might start letting go of whatever is no longer useful to you in your environment first. Cleaning out the closets or drawers works well. What clothes are still hanging around that you haven't worn in a year or no longer fit. What about all the stuff that has been collecting around, are you still using it? If not then the action of clearing what you no longer use or want can be good foundation to build to begin letting go. If you find yourself in a situation where you are in conflict or resistance, practice letting go of whatever it is that is causing the resistance or conflict.

Exercises

In chapter 4 you already gained practice at making your choices consciously and this is a great place to practice recognizing what you want here as well. Take a moment and reflect on what you would like to let go now. Write down whatever it is here.

_____

_____

_____

_____

_____

_____

_____

What do you want to do with the items you are letting go of? It is usually helpful to make a plan of how you want to let go of something.

_____

_____

_____

_____

_____

_____

_____

What have you been trying to control that really wasn't in your grasp to control? What wasn't really yours to control? This may be the hardest place to let go of, and if your experience is anything like mine, this was the place I needed to let go of the most. Spend a moment here in reflection and write about what you are feeling in this moment.

_____

_____

_____

_____

_____

_____

_____

_____

Do you have any issues that you feel blocked or stuck in? Can you surrender the issues? I found it useful to surrender and then go within me and listen for my own guidance in how to maneuver through. Sometimes my guidance was to do nothing and sometimes I needed to take a different step and found it was unique to each situation. What I did need to do each time was to allow the guidance to flow by not trying to answer for it or control when it happened. My action required me to allow and listen. Write about how you feel in this moment.

_____

_____

_____

_____

_____

_____

_____

_____

I also found it helpful to use a statement that was given to me through my inner knowingness. " I unconditionally love the resistance in my desire" and the rest of the statement was based on whatever I was trying to let go of. "I unconditionally love the resistance in my desire to be in alignment with all that I am." You can use this statement with whatever you are trying to let go of by simply inserting whatever it is after "I unconditionally love the resistance in my desire." The statement helped me to get through some of the stickiness of what was around my desire in beliefs and perceptions that were not in my awareness yet. The unconditional love of the resistance allowed it to begin to dissolve and lose some hold on whatever was there. I initially found the words, "unconditional love" a bit intimidating but I do go into more detail of it in the next chapter.

Chapter 10
The Sweetest Love I Have Ever Known

What if you could find a love that was overflowing, happy you just existed, where you were good enough regardless of what experiences you had, what you had done or hadn't done, and loved you unconditionally in all of it? Are you sitting down? Good, you can find the person in your seat. This is the sweet spot and the payoff for all the work you did in the previous chapters. Take a moment and say "I love me". It is within one declaration, one recognition of your love for you, and ready to begin expanding into the relationship with you. How could you not love you? You started seeing you really were doing the best you could in each moment and it is good enough. You had the courage to face your games and the roles you were in and see them for what they were and then make a conscious choice to decide if you still wanted them. You had more courage to begin forgiving others and even more importantly, yourself. You started creating awareness of your choices and started creating ones you actually wanted. You are now understanding what is yours and not carrying the heavy load of others. You have begun going in and tapping into your own inner wisdom. You are feeling what you feel, and yes even your fear while allowing all the parts of you to come back home. You are walking in your own authenticity. You now can let go. You did it and I am impressed and you should be too. You have done so well yet it's not quite time to rest on your laurels. Do you remember me mentioning in the introduction how this was not a destination but a way of life? You now have the tools and they require you to use them daily. The next tool is you recognizing and claiming your own love for yourself.

I began loving me by declaring it. I used affirmations that stated I loved me unconditionally. "I unconditionally love and accept myself in every experience." I first found the words "unconditional love" a bit intimidating until I understood unconditional simply means without conditions. I don't have to do anything, be anything, not do anything or not be anything and I love me regardless. Loving me regardless of what ever is happening around me and I do not have the words to describe the beauty of such a love. I made loving me into a game and explored ways I could show me I loved me daily. I would make inquiries into me and ask myself what could I do today to demonstrate my love for me? The activities would usually be some form of self-care I normally would find myself too busy to do. It might be a long walk that day in nature, a long hot bubble bath, or some delicious dark chocolate I ate all by myself. I started scheduling whatever activity I had come up with for that day on my calendar and I made sure I did it. Each declaration, each self care activity, each love song I sung to myself, each love note I wrote to myself or any other crazy idea I could come up with layered upon one another and added to the building love I was finding from within.

I found the love was already there once I could get through the layers of self incrimination I had built up over the years. I started validating myself and began to look for the validation from me and not outside of me. I can tell you from experience self validation is far more fulfilling than any you can find outside of you. Your own recognition of you can sustain you. Have you ever noticed how when someone else validates you it is short lived? You might be happy in that recognition for a short while but it never lasts. Your own validation does, it is carried with you wherever you go.

I also began to notice a side effect to loving and accepting myself with others. As I could love and accept me, it became much easier to love and accept others. Even if I didn't love them, I could honor they were having their experience and I was having mine. This brings a peace to your life that can hold you in whatever situation you may find yourself in. Life is about experience, some you will like and want to repeat and some you will not. You have a choice, you can see it in love or you can see it any other way you want to. You get to decide how you experience it. You also will begin to notice less emotional reactivity, things can't trigger what is not there.

Can you trust you? Every experience you have had has made you who you are today. There were no wrong choices or wrong paths you took. What you chose, or what action you took brought you to this moment and unfolded through your experiences perfectly. You may not have always liked the experiences but each one was perfect in creating you now. It was all just experience. You cannot do it wrong. Life is here for us to live it, in each moment, and through each experience. Embracing each experience and walking openly and willingly into it allows you to be creator of your life. The trust arrives as you step into you and trust you in each of your experiences. If you don't like what experiences you create, than trust you to know what you like and what you don't and choose again. I do not put my trust in others or in situations. I trust me to trust others or situations as long as they are acting in a trustworthy manner. I also trust me to use discernment and create boundaries with others or situations which do not act trustworthy. I take full ownership of my trust and it stays with me.

If you do find yourself reacting to something, thank it for showing you there is still something there and you know what to do. Go back through the chapters and do a little more work. Remember the words, this is not a destination and you will need to do fine tuning every once in awhile or something may finally emerge that was too deeply entrenched to come out before. It is o.k., you do know what to do. You can trust you, you can accept you, and you can love you.

Exercises

What are some qualities you look for in a friend? How would you want others to treat you? Please reflect on how you want to be treated by others and write as many of the qualities you can.

_____

_____

_____

_____

_____

_____

_____

_____

_____

_____

Treat yourself the way you want others to treat you. Use all the qualities listed above and start practicing treating yourself this way today. Each day reflect on the list and begin to track how often you are treating yourself this way. The activity will begin to change old patterns you might have had of not treating yourself well. Is love important in friendship? What about acceptance and trust? Be your own best friend. Pay attention to how you talk to yourself. Are you using kind words or are they criticizing your actions? Would you want anyone else to talk to you that way? If your words are not kind, change them to how you would want someone else to say the message to you.

What special thing can you do for you today to demonstrate your love for you? Use this inquiry everyday and then do whatever your answer is.

_____

_____

_____

_____

_____

_____

_____

_____

_____

Chapter 11
Relaxation Techniques and Meditations

The deep breath. I have found this to be the most useful of all the tools. The deep breath begins as you inhale through the nose and feel the breath move into your belly. It is important to take the breath all the way down into your stomach and ensure you are not just breathing to your chest area. If it helps place your hand on your stomach and feel the breath move into this area. Then exhale the breath out of the mouth. As you end one breath immediately begin the next breath in a circular motion. I use the deep breath at least 5 minutes in the morning and 5 minutes in the evening. I also use the breath to breathe through any emotions or feelings I might experience and know this helps to integrate and release whatever is there. If you are having difficulties doing the deep breath, try blowing bubbles instead. You have to breathe deeply in order to blow out a bubble from the wand and it may be useful for you.

I keep a bowl of pinto beans in my office for clients to use. Placing your hands in the beans and moving through the beans can be very soothing. If you find difficulty in breathing through a challenging emotion, then try using the deep breath and get a large bowl filled with beans and run your hands through the beans. You also can use squish balls for the same effect.

Practice good self care every day. Taking good care of you is your job and is the way you can feel nurtured and sustained. Self care can be defined in any way you choose. I define it as eating the foods which provide me with the energy I desire and taking good care of me through daily activities. A long walk in nature can revive me from any experiences I might have felt were draining. A long hot bubble bath or eating some dark chocolate is just a few of the ways we can take care of us. Take time to play and laugh. Laughter can shift any mood anytime. What did you find fun at one time but your schedule became too full to allow it? Make the time to start doing it again or start something new. Put yourself first and take care of you. The alternative to putting yourself first will be your reservoir will be drained and you won't have enough of you when you try to help others. My inner wisdom guided me to put myself first and I initially had difficulty doing that. I was a mom and how could I put myself first over my own child. I trusted me and I followed. What I found was a paradox. As I began taking care of me first, I found I had more of me to share with others. I began saying no to a request from another when it interfered with what I wanted in my authentic self. Schedule time just for you daily and use it however you choose to. Use your five senses as much as you can and enjoy the sensations. Smell wonderful scents, taste wonderful tastes, hear wonderful sounds, see beautiful sights, and touch wonderful feels. Are you taking the time to really savor all the tastes of your meal? Do you linger a few moments longer when you smell something really attractive and allow the sensation to embrace you? Are you listening to music you enjoy? Are you finding beauty around you? If you are, wonderful and you are practicing good self care, and if you are not then you can begin at anytime.

The Institute of Heartmath granted me permission to share a simple but powerful technique.

> Create a coherent state in about a minute with the simple, but powerful steps of the Quick Coherence° Technique. Using the power of your heart to balance thoughts and emotions, you can achieve energy, mental clarity and feel better fast anywhere. Use the Quick coherence especially when you begin feeling a draining emotion such as frustration, irritation, anxiety, or anger. Find a feeling of ease and inner harmony that's reflected in more balanced heart rhythms, facilitating brain function and more access to higher intelligence.

1. Focus your attention on the area around your heart, the area in the center of your chest. If you prefer, the first couple of times you try it, place your hand over the center of your chest to help keep your attention in the heart area.

2. Heart Breathing. Breathe deeply but normally and feel as if your breath is coming in and going out your heart area. Continue breathing with ease until you find a natural inner rhythm that feels good to you.

Step 3. Heart Feeling. As you maintain your heart focus and heart breathing, activate a positive feeling. Recall a positive feeling, a time when you felt good inside, and try to re-experience the feeling. One of the easiest ways to generate a positive, heart-based feeling is to remember a special place you've been to or the love you feel for a close friend or family member or treasured pet. This is the most important step.

Create clarity and awareness of what you are paying attention to. What you allow your focus on, whether consciously or by default, will affect how you feel in that moment, or space of time you are in. If you find outside influences feel draining or challenging, then try to shift what you are paying attention to a place which feels better to you. An example of this might be to stop watching the news and listen to some enjoyable music instead. Gratitude and appreciation can shift a state of being very easily. What are you grateful for in your life and what can you appreciate? Many people, objects, situations we have in our life has become so familiar to us we can sometimes forget how blessed we really are. Taking the time to recognize what is there as wells as the appreciation and gratitude for it can be a powerful practice. Recognizing what is yours and what is not will assist you greatly in creating detachment from emotional reactivity to what is in your environment and help you stay neutral. Use compassion with others as much as you can. The compassion is the understanding of what another is experiencing. If someone around you becomes drawn into drama, understand that is their experience, step to the side of it and allow them their experience and choose what you want your experience with them to be.

Meditation can be defined in many ways but I perceive it as connecting into me and practice meditation in many forms. Sometimes I go deeper into me through the method I use and other times I connect in a less deep manner. I find now when I don't take the time to meditate, the next day I feel less centered and grounded. You can use any activity you enjoy where you can stay completely focused only on that activity. I love to sculpt or paint and can completely immerse myself in that activity and find it very meditative. Gardening is also a wonderful way to immerse oneself completely. I also bring my awareness back to me throughout the day. I take a deep breath, feel into me, and let go. This simple exercise has been powerful in allowing my awareness to come back to me and let go of everything else around me. You tube has a wonderful variety of guided meditations that are available for free. The guided meditations are helpful if you find thoughts keep entering your mind and distract you from finding stillness. I enjoy a deep meditation for at least an hour every day in a quiet environment. Meditation is a powerful tool that can be used to connect more into you and find inner stillness. The more you practice meditation the easier it becomes and research has shown it actually changes our brain waves in helpful ways.

The Feel Meditation

Find a quiet environment where you will not be disturbed for whatever length of time you choose. Close your eyes and begin the deep breath. Feel into you in your mind and then the heart. The feel is not a physical action through using your fingers or your hands but just allowing you to feel you. Become aware first of your toes and feel into the toes, then the ball of the feet, heels, ankles, calves, knees and move your way up through your body and feel you as much as you can into each body area. Maintain the deep breath through the entire meditation. When you have moved completely through your body, you can stay there and enjoy the stillness or open your eyes and take another deep breath.

The Let Go Meditation

Find a quiet environment where you will not be disturbed for whatever amount of time you choose. Close your eyes and begin the deep breath. Feel into your mind and find the point your consciousness is fixed at and let go. If you cannot find the point, just feel into your mind and let go from there. Take a deep breath and let go from there again. Keep letting go from where ever you are after you take a deep breath. Let go until you cannot let go anymore. Feel into where you are, and know you have just entered into the deepest part of you, your essence. Stay there for as long as you choose and do remember to keep the breath going.

Level 2 Feel Meditation

Follow the same processes you did for the feel meditation in the beginning of the meditation. Change where you focus your feeling into to your mind and your heart. Try to hold awareness of your mind and your heart at the same time. Don't be concerned if you don't get both the mind and the heart at the same time, it will become easy the more you practice it. Start to feel into you from your heart and mind, and become aware of how it feels. Feel into the feel and stay in this space for as long as you choose and keeping feeling into you. You are feeling your consciousness, or also known as your essence. The more you feel this, the more you bring it into your focus here. Remember to keep the deep breath going the whole time.

Take the quiz now that you have read the book to determine how your perceptions have changed or remained the same. Answer each question with the first response that comes into your mind.

Do you feel ignored when no one is paying attention to you?

Do you feel you have to protect yourself around others?

If you feel someone else has let you down, rejected or betrayed you, do you pull away from everyone else around you as well?

When you are around others do you sometimes act differently depending upon who you are with?

How safe do you feel you can be who you really are around others?

When something upsets you, do you feel tired and/or weak?

Do you feel upset with yourself if you make a mistake?

Do you feel judged by others if you make a mistake?

Do you feel that you cannot trust others?

Do you feel you can trust yourself?

Have you ever felt you had something to share with others but decided not to because you were worried how they would react?

Have you ever had a frustration in your life but you pretended like everything was ok?

Has someone in your life made you feel cold and distant?

Have you felt unsure or insecure about who you are?

When you are getting dressed in the morning what determines what you are going to wear for that day? *1. I want to look good and impress others around me. 2. I want to be comfortable with what I choose?*

Do you believe about yourself *1. I must follow all the rules around me and do what others think I should. 2. I am ok if I am fitting in with the world. 3. I do what I feel is appropriate regardless of what others are doing around me.*

The purpose of my life is *1. I am growing and learning how to be perfect. 2. Embracing each experience 3. Learning how to succeed and fit in with the world around me.*

I believe I am lovable when *1. I have earned someone else's love. 2. I am doing all the right things. 3. I do nothing.*

Conclusion

My inner wisdom guided me to walk openly and willingly into each experience. I only have this moment right now and to stay focused in each moment as it arrives while fully embracing it. To allow and accept every part of me: my mind, emotions, feelings, body, sensations, and all expressions from all parts. The acceptance allows all of me to merge back into me, including my higher self. I found the shadow aspects of me were not shadows at all but it was my perceptions of them which were actually shadowed. Each of them was serving me the best they could from what they were and I now can see such beauty in that. They were willing to go where I did not want to and did so with courage. Each experience carries the potentials for love, understanding, acceptance and the clarity of who I am in that experience. This is true for all of us.

About the Author

 My name is Lisa McTavis. I am a Licensed Clinical Social Worker and I work at an agency as a mental health counselor. The work I do as a counselor is to connect clients back into them and support them in finding their own acceptance and love for themselves. It is my passion. I live in sunny New Mexico with my 17 year old daughter. I also enjoy oil painting and sculpting. www://journeyintolovingyou.com

Glossary

Feeling into you

Creating a moment wherein you are able to connect with your thoughts, feelings, and sensations to identify if it resonates with you or is out of alignment with you. Feel is also identified as a form of awareness in you and a sensory perception. Example: the feel of a room when you first walk in.

Give it the light of day

We observe ourselves, others, and the world around us and then process that data through our minds. The mind does the best it can to interpret the data to protect us and keep us safe. At times the data can be misinterpreted and something can appear to be something it is not. The action of expressing a belief, perception, or emotions through journaling or discussing it with another allows us to bring it out of the mind and explore what meaning has been attached to it and then explore what other alternatives we might want. Creating the awareness of whatever is there is the first step in allowing us to gain more clarity around it and then decide what we want.

Integration

Allowing all the parts and pieces of someone that have been rejected and pushed away, to return back home to merge back into the person. When we do not feel what we feel or do not like how our feelings communicate, we can push them away. The integration of those feelings allows them to merge back with us and release the emotional charge they were carrying.

Letting go

Releasing your grasp or control over anything. As well as the conscious decision to no longer allow someone, something to have power or influence over you.

Narrative, Reality, Mindfulness and Existentialism Therapy

Theories and approaches based in psychology by various practitioners. There are many theories available and each one uses a particular structure to understand and explain human thought, emotions, or behavior.

Surrender

Releasing something to your higher power. The conscious decision to be willing to allow and receive help.

Test of Truth

The action of looking for any evidence to see if it is what it appears to be or it is something else. We can get caught in a trap in the mind through accepting and believing how the mind perceives the world around us as truth. The mind works very hard for each one of us and uses all of our experiences and how we perceived them at the time to process new data coming in. Some of these perceptions could have been accurate when tested against the evidence or some of them might not have been. It is helpful for us to create as much clarity around our perceptions we can and an easy way to achieve this is to look for any evidence to see if it is true.

Validation

A manner in which individuals derive a sense of worth, acceptance or importance.

Resources

A website is available to compliment this book at http://journeyintolovingyou.com I will be updating the website continuously. I will also post youtube videos that can be accessed from youtube or the website which offers simulations through roleplays on some of the techniques in the book and meditations. I will have graphic organizers available for free on the website that can support you in using some of the techniques, as well as various quizzes.

Journey into Loving You has a facebook page available.

Bibliography

Hall, Dr. Yvonne, interview by Lisa McTavis LMSW. (2013).

Institute of HeartMath. www.heartmath.org. (accessed 2013).

Wilner, Joe LMLP. *PsychCentral, Adventures in Positive Psychology.* http://blogs. psychcentral.com/positive-psychology/2011/09/how-to-break-your-worry-habit- and-overcome-anxiety/#more-1471 (accessed 2013).

Index

I

illusion 44, 49
inner wisdom 36
integrating 24, 44
intention ix, 20, 32, 33, 35
interconnected 1, 27

J

journaling 6
judging 6, 20, 24, 51

L

layering 37, 45
let go 14, 15, 32, 49, 50, 51, 52, 53, 54, 55, 62, 63
the light of day 28, 29, 30, 71
love vii, viii, xi, xiii, xvi, 1, 32, 40, 54, 55, 56, 57, 58,
    61, 62, 65, 67, 69

M

meditation 62
mindfulness 39, 72
mistakes 17, 20, 37

N

narrative therapy 30

O

observer role 38
outside influences 1, 2, 3, 4, 61

P

patterning 6, 14
peace 9
perception 10, 14, 15, 20, 32, 33, 39, 40, 45, 47, 49,
    51, 71
present moment 47

R

reality therapy 25
reject 40
relationship 1, 27, 33, 49, 55
relaxation 11
resistance 49, 50, 51, 52, 54
roles 9, 31, 34, 49, 55

S

sadness 45
safe space 11
self-care 56
sensations 40, 41, 45, 46, 60, 67, 71
shame 6, 18, 45
surrender 50, 53
sympathy 30

T

test of truth 27
trauma 11, 39
trust xv, 33, 50, 57, 58, 64
truth xiii, 10, 27, 28, 30, 31, 40, 44, 72

U

unconditional xiii, 54, 56
unconditionally love 54

V

validation vii, xiii, xiv, 56
victim game 10, 11

W

wisdom ix, 18, 24, 31, 32, 33, 36, 37, 55, 67
worthy vii, 22, 51